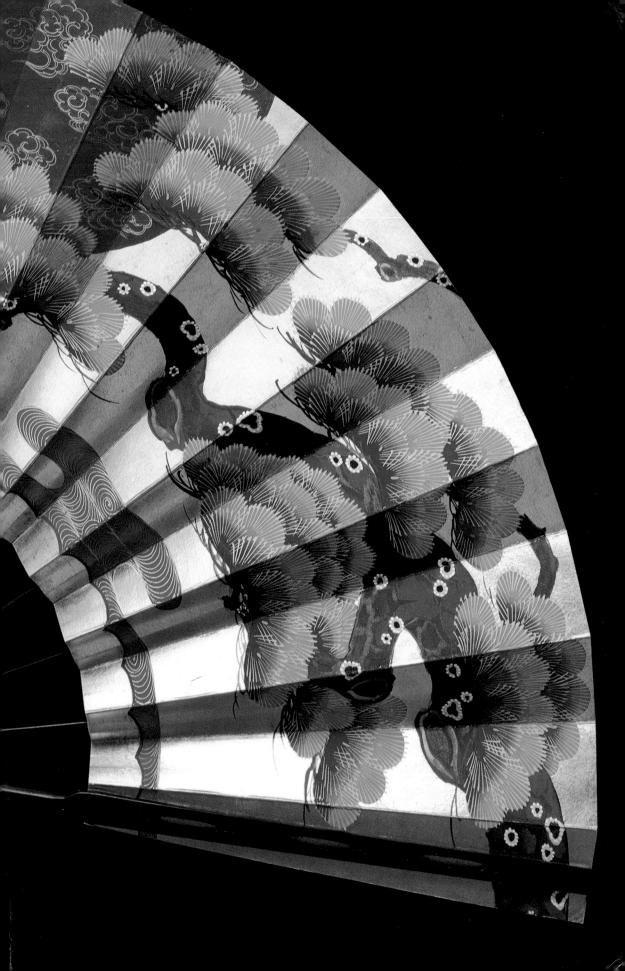

The Compact Culture

Published by Toyo Kogyo Co., Ltd.,
Hiroshima, Japan.

THE COMPACT CULTURE

The Ethos of Japanese Life

Edited by Yoshida Mitsukuni, Tanaka Ikko & Sesoko Tsune

Covers: The fan, shown partially open on the
cover and fully open on different sides on the
inside front and inside back covers, is of
the type used in the noh dance called *shimai*
(performed without mask or noh costume).
The folding fan (as opposed to Chinese fans
that do not fold) was first created in the
Heian period (794 – 1185) is one of the best
examples of the Japanese affinity for
compactness.
The fan illustrated has eight bamboo ribs
which the fan maker deftly inserts between
prepared sheets of paper in one motion.
This does not include the ribs at each end
whose patterns (in the case of noh fans) vary
according to the different schools of noh.
The hand-painted design of the fan on the
inside front cover shows pines against a
rising sun. The design on the inside back
cover is of whitecaps against a setting sun.

The Japanese names in this book are given
last name first in the customary Japanese order.

Contents

The Ethos of Japanese Life

by Yoshida Mitsukuni

In the course of Japan's history, the first recognizable outlines of the culture as we know it today emerge in the Tokugawa period. This was a peaceful age, spanning some two-hundred and seventy years between medieval times and the dawn of the modern period. Throughout that time, the country's territory neither expanded nor decreased, and its population remained almost stable at about 30 million.

Such an unusual period of peace depended on conditions that were created by a policy of isolation imposed by the feudal society that ruled from the early seventeenth to the late nineteenth century. The policy was carried out with remarkable, and severe, consistency. It prohibited all contact with other countries except China, Korea, and Holland, and relations with these three were limited exclusively to trade. All foreign commerce was confined to the port of Nagasaki. The quantity of trade was carefully controlled, so that the goods imported had little effect on the domestic economy. Insular Japan grew all the more introverted, while the economy became totally self sufficient. The only communication with the world came through Nagasaki, via the handful of Dutch traders permitted by the shogun to live in Nagasaki and travel to the capital at Edo at prescribed times. One of them, Engelbert Kaempfer (1651–1716), wrote one of the first works introducing Japan to the West, *History of Japan*. In view of its unique economy and culture, Kaempfer concluded, seclusion was the most reasonable and natural choice for the nation.

Feudal Japan under the Tokugawa shoguns was made up of some 300 fiefs of varying sizes, each governed by a provincial lord who ran it as a semi-autonomous domain. People were not encouraged to move around, and few had to, for the domains were self-sufficient economic units. Most people, in fact, passed their entire lives without once leaving the area where they were born. The world as they knew it was defined by the small community immediately surrounding them.

This terraced rice cultivation in land-scarce Japan shows attention to detail usually associated with gardening.

The land that shaped their imagination and experience, moreover, was largely forest-covered mountains, for the area that could be cultivated was very small. Even today some 70 percent of the land is either forest or wilderness; in premodern times that proportion was even larger. In order to get everything they could out of the precious little arable soil available to them, farmers devised a unique system of cultivation that was so intensive and painstaking that it resembled gardening more than farming. They rarely used draft animals, but relied on manpower for the chief tasks of agriculture. They refined their techniques for coaxing the largest possible harvest from the earth and carried on only minimal stock farming.

The climate in the islands of Japan, which stretch out in a long north-south arc along the continent, varies greatly depending on the latitude. While most countries lie in a single climatic zone, Japan encompasses the range of climates from subarctic to subtropical. Japanese wet rice agriculture developed over the centuries in response to this varied natural setting, and farmers had to adapt their own techniques to the particular climatic conditions of their region.

The well-defined political and economic divisions in the feudal society and the diverse natural characteristics of each region heightened people's awareness of locality. They encouraged people to turn inward and focus their attention on their own surroundings, rather than affairs outside their community or province. A centripetal pattern of thinking gradually dominated society, and the family, the first group with which a person identifies, became the central reference for human relations.

Wet rice cultivation requires intensive labor at certain times, which a single family alone can not provide. The families in a community learned to pool their labor, concentrating available manpower to fulfill the needs of planting and harvesting. This pattern of communal agricultural activity created strong community solidarity, whose legacy remains today in the emphasis on small groups in the Japanese concept of man and society.

Nature was at once bountiful, cruel, and unpredictable to these people, and their livelihood depended on it. To palliate its excesses, particularly when the rugged land they worked was so difficult to cultivate to begin with, they performed regular rites to a complex pantheon of animistic deities. They believed that spirits dwelled in the various attributes of nature and in all things, and they recognized a special power in each spirit. They gave concrete form to the spirits, which they worshiped as deities. Among the most important were the spirits of their ancestors, to whom the living paid special homage in return for protection and blessings.

Unlike cultures in which the absolute is regarded as something abstract and transcendental, Japanese culture identified absoluteness with the real phenomena of mundane human existence. While Western philosophy and

Ground-breaking Shinto ceremony, with altar set up within an area, representing the *kekkai* sacred boundary

religion, for example, tend to relegate the absolute or the divine to a single god or a small number of beings, Japanese animism recognizes divinity in all things. Thus, the countless shrines, large and small, that dot the landscape of Japanese life may look similar, but they each enshrine a different deity.

For each function or occasion, people select the appropriate one to honor from among the countless deities, for there is no almighty god. The power of each deity is measured by the benefits it confers, and so Japanese pray to one when they become sick, to another for a good harvest, and to yet another when they want to be married. The indigenous gods are functional gods.

As if the plethora of functional gods were not enough, Japanese also became Buddhists. Developing in India, Buddhism offered a way to transcend the phenomenal world in search of man's original and essential being. After it reached Japan from China in the sixth century, however, Buddhism was transformed. The emphasis was shifted to man in the phenomenal world in search of a transcendental realm. Thus, in Japan, Buddhism too became a religion that affirmed the phenomenal world. Buddhist altars are a common fixture in the Japanese household. They enshrine the souls of the family ancestors, which are elevated to divine status and honored in regular ceremonies. They are, in effect, shrines of ancestor worship centering around the image of the Buddha. In addition, most households also keep a household shrine to honor the indigenous gods that bring happiness to the family and protect the home.

Responding to the vicissitudes of a diverse land and climate, enduring the hardships brought by storms and floods, and living close to the mountains and forests that surrounded them, Japanese grew skillful at adapting their way of life to their natural environment. In this environment the rhythms of daily living and patterns of behavior took shape.

The large rhythmic pattern of life is described by the concepts of *hare* and *ke. Hare* refers to what might be called the nodes in a person's life, times that are special or extraordinary or momentous and are recognized formally and socially. A child's birth is his first personal *hare* occasion, and it is duly much celebrated. When he enters the first grade, this too is a *hare* event, and family and friends send him gifts to mark this high point. Other *hare* occasions include graduation from school, finding one's first job, promotion, and marriage. Family and friends celebrate each such occasion, helping the person to recognize the significance of that step as one of the numerous checkpoints he must pass through before he achieves completeness as a person. *Ke* refers to the periods between *hare* events. Ideally these intervals should be calm and peaceful times in the flow of life.

This lake-and-island style garden was built to create a sacred place where one could indulge in immortal daydreams.

The continuum of *hare* and *ke* is a natural rhythm, not only in human life but in time itself. Thus the New Year is celebrated as an important *hare* occasion, just as the special times in a person's life are. People don their best formal clothes and prepare special festive foods. Other *hare* moments in the year are the seasonal festivals related to the agricultural and fishing cycles, the festival of the local shrine, and the family occasions honoring the ancestors. The rhythm of *hare* occasions helps to mark the passage of time throughout the year and it encourages appreciation of the peaceful, less eventful periods of *ke* that lie between them.

Just as time is a continuum of *hare* and *ke*, space is a mingling of *sei* and *zoku*, or sacred and profane. Spirits were believed to abide in the seas, mountains, rivers, forests and fields; their dwelling places were considered sacred and it was taboo to disturb them in any way. Even today, shrines dedicated to *nogami* (spirits of the fields) may be found in fields and paddies all over the country.

The house, too, has its sacred spaces. In the traditional home, there is always a *tokonoma*, usually a recessed alcove set apart from the area where the activities of daily life go on. During most of the year, the *tokonoma* is adorned with a hanging picture scroll and an arrangement of flowers, both designed to evoke the appropriate season. On *hare* occasions, however, the *tokonoma* is transformed to become a kind of sacred space. The scrolls used on ordinary days are replaced with special ones bearing auspicious scenes or calligraphy. The flower arrangement, too, has festive meaning. At New Year's, for example, balls of soft pounded rice (*mochi*) are placed there. It is believed that the gods that bring happiness visit each home at New Year's and the *mochi* is intended as gifts for them. The *tokonoma* becomes sacred during those few days by virtue of its temporary function as a hospice for the gods. In the past, whenever a *hare* event approached, the whole house became sacred. That tradition is recalled today by the practice of hanging *shimenawa* (rice straw cord with strips of white paper) at the entrance of homes at New Year's, just as it marks the sacred precincts of a shrine. Since ancient times the *shimenawa* has been a symbol demarcating sacred space, and so when it is hung at the entrance of a home, it signifies the sanctity of the whole house. In this way the life of a household itself enters the continuum of the sacred and the profane, and by a simple symbolic action the profane may be transformed into the sacred and the sacred into the profane.

The Buddhist household altar is also a sacred space. As such, it is usually adorned with golden ornaments and often contains a golden figure of the Buddha as well, for gold is the color of the sun and of the sacred and mystic. The use of gold was most lavish in Buddhist temples, while in homes it was usually confined to the Buddhist altar. The gold of the Buddha figure reflects the traditional belief that the Buddha himself glowed with a golden aura.

Because gold sanctifies space, the folding screen set up for wedding ceremonies and on New Year's Day is gold. It functions to transform space for a *hare* event. Standing behind a newly married couple, a gold screen sanctifies a festive occasion. But it is temporary. When it is folded up and put away, the space returns to its former everyday role—the sacred reverts to the profane for another interval.

Another sacred space that developed under the influence of Chinese Taoism is the Japanese landscape garden, whose roots lie far back in history, around the seventh century. Taoist beliefs recognize a world of supernatural beings (*shen-hsien*) that dwell in nature apart from human society. They are ageless and immortal, and live simply by breathing nature's essences, the mists and dew. The home of the *shen-hsien* was believed to be three "divine mountains" or islands rising out of the "eastern sea" off China. The Taoist ideal was to become one of these immortal beings and live eternally in their idyllic land. Chinese sought to recreate this utopia in miniature to provide a refuge from this-worldly cares. The Han dynasty emperors landscaped gardens within their palace grounds in the likeness of the "divine mountains," and these became the model on which the Japanese nobility, who emulated so many aspects of Chinese art and culture, built their own gardens. Building islands in broad ponds, they, too, recreated the mythical islands rising out of the "eastern sea."

The garden with a lake and islands became the prototype in Japan. Bridges were built to the islands, and pavilions provided for the leisure hours of wealthy aristocrats, who enjoyed daydreams of being transformed to the land of immortality. Japanese have always believed that large, irregularly shaped rocks are places where the gods rest. When they built their garden islands, they used stones, and in this they were quietly imposing their own beliefs onto the construction and design of the garden-image of the Chinese mythical land. To the legends and mystical beliefs that lay behind the principles of landscape gardening were added yet another layer when Buddhist concepts became popular. The Buddhist paradise is a bright, beautiful realm, and so Japanese added trees and ·shrubs to the idyllic Taoist mountain scene, making it a pleasant world of imagination and fantasy.

The central rocks in these gardens also acquired names associated with Buddhism, such as *sanzon-seki* (lit., rocks of the "three honorable ones") after the Buddhist triumvirate. By the twelfth century, the characteristic elements of the Japanese garden, combining a lake and island, had been perfected.

Around the end of the ninth century, Japan ceased sending envoys to the imperial court in China and contact with the continent grew more and more infrequent. As direct Chinese influences faded and Japanese culture began to develop aesthetic models of its own, the prototype for the landscape garden changed from the Taoist dwelling place of immortal spirits to scenic landscapes noted in literature. Whereas Chinese verse (*kanshi*) had monopolized the prominent place in the literary world, now *waka*, poems written in the Japanese vernacular, became the center of the short verse genre.

The themes of *waka* were strictly Japanese. In time, the literary elite in the capital became better informed about the diverse landscape of the country. The vast differences in climate and culture in different parts of the country had created great variety in the regional landscape. The poets at the imperial court drew on reports about the landscape to develop imaginary landscapes that were so exquisite as to represent conceptual ideals. Gradually people became convinced that poetic landscapes created in literature actually existed.

Like the Taoist land of immortality, they were models of imaginary realms, well suited to landscape garden designs, which could reduce entire universes to a scale comprehensible to the human senses. To stroll in such a garden was to be transported to the vast and peaceful beauties of these idealized worlds.

The gardens were not simply reduced versions of the landscape. They were attempts, rather, at recreating as faithfully as possible—and in the compact proportions appropriate to a garden—the impression of a noted landscape in literature. The vast universe of space in nature represented by the landscape was compressed into the space available. Thus the basic principle of garden design became the creation of a microcosm that corresponded aesthetically to the macrocosm of the natural landscape.

In China, particularly during the T'ang dynasty, it became a popular practice to create a garden, modeled after the paradise of immortal beings, on such a small scale that one could have access to it any time. The murals of ancient tombs tell us what such miniature gardens were like. A number of stones were arranged in a shallow, round or oval dish and two or three plants tucked between them. The murals show people holding such pots in their hands, which indicates that they were very small. These were the early bonsai.

Selecting the stones for these miniature gardens became an art that demanded great skill in discriminating the valuable. Specific stones with unusual shapes were especially prized. Chinese T'ai-hu stones were much sought after. They were blocks of limestone formed in eccentric shapes that came from the area of T'ai-hu, a large lake located between Kiangsu and Chekiang provinces. These little gardens gave rise to another form that

This river stone, small enough to hold in the hand, evokes an image of mountains. It is macrocosm in microcosm.

became widespread during the Sung and Ming dynasties, the *bonseki*, which literally means "tray stones." Several small, carefully chosen stones were arranged on a tray meant to be placed indoors. The viewer was encouraged to see in it a natural setting, taking cues from the shape of the stones. Some of the stones used in *bonseki* became quite famous among connoisseurs of this miniature art. With shapes evoking the undulating lines of linked mountain ridges, they could carry those who gazed at them to the vastness of the natural landscape. One such rock was called the "Nine Flowers." It referred to a mountain in Shenhsi province called Huashang, "the flower mountain," whose many ridges are likened to the petals of a flower. Because of that stone, a specific natural landscape could be reproduced in the space of a small pot. Another, called "Sky Caverns," contained a number of natural "caverns" that opened upwards as if directly linked with the skies. The owner of this rock set it on an attractive wooden tray filled with incense so that the fragrance seemed to drift out of the openings in the stone. These were the fruit of fantasies about the world of immortal beings. A great many books on such noted stones appeared, one describing as many as 116 different examples, including garden rocks, tray stones, and inkstones. Each was a miniature representation of the universe. Porcelain trays were made to set off *bonseki*, adding the beauty and variety of China's highly developed ceramic art to these capsules of landscape.

Bonsai and *bonseki* were introduced to Japan sometime around the twelfth century when contact with the continent was resumed. The oldest known record of miniature landscape art in Japan is the picture scroll, *Saigyo monogatari*, which was painted at the end of the twelfth century. The scroll shows the poet Saigyo (1118-90) at a temple in Kyoto, about to set out upon his journeys. A large rectangular tray supported by two posts stands at the edge of the temple veranda, and on the tray is a strangely shaped stone with several miniature trees growing on it. Another illustration is found in the *Kasuga gongen kenkie*, a 20-volume picture scroll recounting the history and miracles of the Kasuga Grand Shrine in Nara. In a vivid drawing of the garden of the prominent poet and leading court noble, Fujiwara no Shunzei, there is an elaborate shelf on the veranda bearing a tray filled with a diminutive landscape of oddly-shaped rocks, miniature shrubs, and blooming trees, and surrounded with a covering of white sand planted with sweet flag. The scene also shows what appears to be a green porcelain bowl with stones and sweet flag in bloom. As might be expected of the garden of a Heian aristocrat, these are particularly splendid examples, demonstrating that Japanese men of learning, like their Chinese counterparts, had discovered the pleasures of imagining the vastness of the universe in the small world of bonsai.

The sweets, protected from the "defiled" *tatami* by the tray, are placed on the *kaishi* paper which also provides "purity

As later picture scrolls depicting bonsai show, the vessels themselves grew more and more beautiful. All were imported ceramics from China, for porcelain-making techniques in Japan lagged behind considerably. Fine ceramics from China were immensely prized by members of the court, as well as by Zen monks, many of whom were in direct contact with China through trade.

In Japan, as in China, appreciation of stones themselves became a kind of cult. The Emperor Godaigo (1288–1339), who lived a life beset by constant political turmoil, was a particular connoisseur of stones. Forced by political strife and war to flee Kyoto, he included among the treasures he carried away from the capital a famed stone which had been brought from China called the "Floating Bridge of Dreams." Taken from the title of one chapter of the Heian period classic, *The Tale of Genji*, the name recalls a bridge that connects heaven and earth. This stone survives today.

Another stone preserved today at the Sanjusangendo temple in Kyoto was a favorite of the mid-fifteenth century shogun Ashikaga Yoshimasa, whose power was second only to the emperor, and who was also a connoisseur of stones. It was called "Magnificent Mountain," and indeed, is exactly like an immense mountain in miniature.

"Sue-no-Matsuyama" was yet another illustrious rock of a later period. Its name, taken from a classical verse, evoked a range of mountains seen from afar. "Sue-no-Matsuyama" originally belonged to Oda Nobunaga (1534-82), the warrior who began the process of unifying Japan, and it is now in the keeping of Nishi Honganji temple in Kyoto. To find a stone that could be held in the palm of a hand and to let it sweep the imagination off into the vastness of nature—this was one way men of power diverted themselves. And they were moved by much the same impulse as those who sought some echo of the world of immortal beings through the medium of a garden.

Lapidary tastes in Japan gradually diverged from the preference among Chinese for peculiar shapes to gentle, soft contours reminiscent of the typical Japanese mountain landscape. The shape that came to be most highly valued was a naturally formed cone like the silhouette of Mt. Fuji, and the best size was about 15-20 centimeters wide at the base and 12-15 centimeters high. Rocks carved or artifically shaped in any way were inadmissible for use as *bonseki*. River stones were considered superior, while stones from the mountains or coastal areas were avoided. Once the right stone was found, it was set on an oval, black lacquered tray called a *katsura-bon*, without decoration. The area around the stone was covered with sand. *Bonseki* were usually displayed in the *tokonoma*, and great care was taken to bring out the proper harmony between the stone and the painting or calligraphy on the hanging scroll.

The governing elite of Japan tended to favor bonsai, also. Ashikaga Yoshimasa was no less a connoisseur of bonsai than of *bonseki*, and he collected many fine examples from temple collections in Kyoto, selecting only those he loved most. The aesthete Iemitsu, third Tokugawa shogun who ruled in the mid-seventeenth century, was especially attached to his bonsai. He usually kept a tiny pine tree next to his bed at night. Two of Iemitsu's treasured pine tree bonsai which have survived are now more than three hundred years old.

During the long, peaceful centuries of the Tokugawa period, the feudal order grew rigid and the ranks of the leisure class grew. Confined socially and geographically, the wealthy in particular felt the need for some link to the wider universe. Landscape gardening, bonsai, and *bonseki* fulfilled this need. They were developed to a high art, and they stimulated the publication of numerous manuals on cultivation and forms, as well as illustrated catalogues. Techniques for cultivating bonsai, including ways to make relatively young, small trees look old, became highly refined, and various stereotypical forms were established. Bonsai and *bonseki* fairs as well as contests were a frequent occurrence in the cities.

Around the middle of the nineteenth century, visitors from Western countries began coming to Japan. To them, the concepts of Japanese landscape gardening, bonsai, and similar arts that had developed within the historical and social milieu of the Edo period, were difficult to understand. Josiah Condor, an Englishman who introduced modern Western architecture to Japan, wrote in his book *Landscape Gardening in Japan* (1912) that Japanese and European gardening were completely different in basic principles as well as techniques. Japanese gardening is an art, he said, while Western gardening is a science. The former represents nature, the latter geometry. Understanding began in 1901 when the Japan Society in London held a lecture on bonsai, and a year later, when forty-seven bonsai were taken to England, all were sold immediately.

Just as they found ways to create sacred space even on the smallest scale, Japanese constantly searched the phenomenal world for affirmation of their existence in terms of its relation with the universe. Bonsai and *bonseki* are good examples of that pursuit.

Japanese believed that all things were endowed with spirit. According to traditional beliefs, the universe is vertically divided into three worlds: heaven, earth, and hell. Heaven is called Takama-no-hara, a realm filled with light and the dwelling place of myriad gods. Hell is the world of darkness, populated by numerous evil spirits. Earth, which lies between heaven and hell, is the home of man, and there light, daytime and good, the divine elements of heaven, come together and mingle with darkness, night, and wickedness, the evil elements of hell. The many spirits that reside within the things of earth are linked with the gods in heaven.

Surrounded on earth by the forces of good and evil, and light and darkness, man must constantly obey the will of the heavenly deities and strive to communicate with them. This concern is expressed in the tradition of putting up a tall pole during festivals. The pole is a signal to the gods, who are guided by it when they descend to earth bearing messages of happiness—as long as people observe their will. This is part of a set of beliefs based on the concept of *kegare*, or defilement. Death and blood are considered *kegare*, and fixed amounts of time and purificatory rites were traditionally considered necessary before it could be eliminated. The taboo represented by *kegare* was so strong that even regular court functions were cancelled or postponed in ancient times until it had passed.

In Japan today, while there are still numerous shrines dedicated to all manner of gods, there is no tradition of sacrificial rites. Religious sacrifice was performed in cultures throughout the world, and among the Maya of Mexico and other agricultural peoples, it was an important religious rite. No such practice developed in Japan, or if it did, it died out, probably because Japanese traditionally consider death and blood to be defilement.

Kegare is not a fixed state, but may be transmuted to its opposite, purity (*sei*), through the medium of ritual. An example of this metamorphosis may be observed in the tea ceremony. When a guest is served a sweet, he takes out a piece of thick rice-paper (*kaishi*) from a folded packet and places it on the *tatami* mat, transferring the sweet from the serving dish to the paper. As part of the prescribed ritual, he must refold the paper inside out so that the sweet rests on the side of the paper that was protected. This may appear to be simply a matter of sanitation, since the *tatami* is walked upon. But in fact, this rule grows out of the concept of defilement—the symbolic defilement associated with something over which the feet of people have passed. The paper, its fresh inside turned out, spread upon the *tatami* creates a purified place for the sweet that is both ritually and literally clean.

The *tatami* of a Japanese house is not always considered to be defiled. Contrasted with the earth itself, it is pure. Upon entering the house, it is customary to remove one's shoes, which carry the dirt and the defilement of the ground. To remove one's shoes is to prevent *kegare* from entering the house.

The soil is believed to be the preserve of the earth deity, who has different characteristics and names depending on the region. As a rule, it is fierce and powerful, and has no compunctions about bringing on disaster, which is the source of the belief that the earth is *kegare*. Thus any human action that affects the earth must be accompanied by rituals to soothe its irascible deity.

One million of these three-storied stupas filled with dharani were made in the 8th century for the temples of Japan.

Construction of a building, for example, calls for prescribed rituals. First a *shimenawa* or sacred cord is stretched around the site, demarcating the space to be purified. Within, a temporary altar is set up and rites are held petitioning the god of the earth to permit the building and explaining that it is not an evil deed. Once this ritual has been completed, the god of the earth becomes the guardian deity of the building, protecting it and the people within it.

This custom also demonstrates the transformation of *kegare* into *sei*, when defilement changes into purity, and evil is converted to good. The transformation is smooth as long as people observe the will of the gods. The same continuity that underlies the interaction of the sacred and the profane and *hare* and *ke* applies to defilement and purity. Again, the distinction between defiled and pure is not absolute; they can be trans-formed through the manipulation—or neglect—of symbols or ritual.

It is tempting to conclude that the core of Japanese culture is dualistic. In a sense it is, but the opposite elements are not such that they clash or work to eliminate each other. In Japan, the two sides complement each other and can be transformed into one another, simply through the intervention of human will and initiative.

This kind of dualism became rooted in Japanese thinking in a more concrete and realistic form than the dualism of Chinese philosophy. It might be described as an elaborated pattern of the yin/yang dialectic: at the core of the circle is the human being, and the microcosm created from his life experience is represented by a smaller circle, its size differing from person to person. The microcosmic world, and the macrocosmic also, are laid over by the dualism of the defiled and the pure. The smaller circle is the immediate reality of everyday life; the bigger circle the world as perceived by man.

The complex of macrocosm and microcosm symbolize the way that Japanese, by adapting themselves to their small land and learning to cope with the diversity of regional climates, have cultivated, is a world on the smallest possible scale. In their confined world, the idea that two things are not opposed to one another, but are linked, is very helpful. Shifting like a Möbius band, the realm of the sacred yields to the world of the profane, and the special high points of *hare* occasions give way to the calm stability of everyday life.

The whole Japanese way of life absorbs change and versatility into its organic rhythm. What wonder, then, that they devised things that could be transformed from the one-dimensional to the three-dimensional, or vice versa.

The Mandala of Japanese Dualism

Expressions of the Compact Culture

by Yoshida Mitsukuni

Flexibility, love of symbols, small size—these are all qualities that accompany the proclivity towards compactness in Japanese culture. They developed and have been refined to an unusual level in Japan partly out of the necessity to use limited space economically, but these qualities also characterize the aesthetic preferences of the people. Because space is so precious, it receives a great deal of attention in every aspect of life. Over the centuries Japanese have devised innumerable ways to use space that are ingenious in their successful combination of pragmatism, harmony, and beauty. Folding, stacking, rolling, nesting, carrying, consolidating, miniaturizing, and transforming are some of the techniques for living that have created the compact culture. Each one is put to use in countless ways, suggesting principles and conceptions that encapsulate the wisdom of tradition. (*Ed.*)

Folding allows a one-dimensional object to be placed in a prescribed small space. A large, flat sheet, folded over on itself, surrenders nothing of its nature for the sake of size. Even a three-dimensional object, like a paper lantern, yields form to space when folded, but it is only put aside until needed. By unfolding, it is brought back to life to function once more, its beauty resurrected. A kimono, which is sewn of many flat pieces, can be folded neatly, without a wrinkle, to lie inert in a drawer until it is worn and regains its three-dimensional vitality. Unfolding a golden screen, also, releases its power to transform an ordinary, informal space into sacred space. Folded, its mystic function withdraws.

Stacking objects of the same shape makes use of vertical space, saving valuable horizontal space. Stacking is practical, but the action of piling or unpiling objects also gives them the added beauty of movement. Stacking objects integrates them into a three-dimensional, sculptural form; unstacking them revives the individuality and autonomy of each unit. For practical use, the three-dimensional form must be dismantled, and by the manipulation of human hands, static beauty is made dynamic. A pile of graduated saké cups is an elegant form, but its function is dormant. Only when saké is poured into the uppermost cup and served, then into the next, and so on, do the parts come into their own as they are separated from the integrated form and scattered in many directions.

Rolling an object reduces it to a tidy cylinder without creasing it, creating yet another form of repose for functionally flat things. Part of the charm of rolling things is in the unrolling. When pulled out, they gradually reveal the different and the new, as in a Japanese scroll painting (*emaki*). In this long, one-dimensional art, the landscape and the narrative move from scene to scene in an unbroken flow. While the  past can be rolled away to rest, it can be recalled anytime by unrolling. The beauty of kimono fabric, too, lies dormant in the bolt of cloth, waiting to be unrolled and brought to life when the kimono is sewn. Rolling makes possible a continuous alternation of withdrawal and emergence that is in itself graphically interesting, while it is also a practical and common method of organizing things in limited space. That vital item to keep out the heat of summer, the bamboo shade (*sudare*), can be rolled up into a small cylinder for the rest of the year. Rolling different things together is a technique well-loved by connoisseurs of the culinary arts also: by rolling, various flavors, textures, colors are mingled, producing yet new tastes.

Nesting several identically shaped objects of graduated sizes is known as *ireko*. Sets of traditional square measuring boxes (*masu*) are often nested this way, creating a centripetal figure reminiscent of the geometrically beautiful forms of Plato's universe. The concentric lines of nested alms bowls on the other hand, evoke the ancient Chinese conception of heaven—hemispherical layers oriented to a common center overarching earth. It seems fitting that these implements, intended to receive the tokens of solidarity among people, should symbolize in form the archetypal images of Eastern thought. Then, too, the graduated lines of the square *masu* remind us of the primitive form of the Pyramids. But more than symbols, these are items of practical function, and wherever objects of identical shape and varied size are used, the mystic symmetry of the world of *ireko* emerges. Consecutively larger worlds embrace the smaller, and the smaller open out upon ever larger worlds; thus man interacts with the universe, and his life converges with it.

Carrying things by hand makes them available for any occasion, by plan or on impulse. For people everywhere in the world, the magic box that yields up anything the heart desires holds undying fascination. The *tebako* is the mundane version of the magic box, a small, portable case furnished to fulfill one's every need. In the art of enjoying life, portability has long been an important asset. The early masters of the tea ceremony, for example, devised tidy and tastefully designed cases equipped with all the necessary utensils so that they could perform the tea ceremony anywhere. Then and today, the pleasure of an outing is enhanced when all the implements for eating and drinking are provided, and the occasion is savored more if the furnishings are beautiful, each serving its special purpose. The wisdom and tradition that gave birth to the arts of portability is very much alive in the accouterments of modern life.

Consolidating is to bring together the multifarious systems of living into an integrated whole. In the routines of daily life—even the occasional diversion—each has its own order, and together they make up our day-to-day experience. Living in a small, crowded land, Japanese developed a habit of ordering each system and its functional requirements into a careful arrangement and small space. The implements of a game invariably come in a set compactly designed to fit a given space. A game or diversion is a system that is autonomous and separate from daily routine; its beginning and end are explicit, and it must always be concluded to have meaning. To be true to its purpose, moreover, a game needs excitement and intensity. It begins when the magic box with all the implements is opened, and ends when they are put away. In replacing them, a full cycle of one of life's systems is completed—the start and the end of human activity in microcosm.

Miniaturizing things is a way to bring even the universe down to the scale of a human hand. Because man himself is one particular universe—a miniature version of the infinite universe that surrounds him—a subtle bond joins the microcosm of man to the macrocosm of the universe. Cultures all over the world have known of this relationship from ancient times, and it was applied to the worlds people discovered and created themselves. They believed that by creating microcosms of their own, they could actually experience the bond with the macrocosm. The life system of the emperor, a sacred being, was symbolic of the ideal of all life systems. Thus, by creating a tiny model of that ideal system, people believed they assured happiness for themselves. This is the notion behind the miniature doll-world created for the Doll's Festival.

The principles of Japanese landscape gardening, as well as *bonseki* and bonsai, grow out of the same urge to forge links with the universe. A miniature landscape provides a medium to experience the mysterious and the divine, a utopia controlled by a transcendental being. Within such a reduced setting, a person can sense the presence of the divine. Trees and plants are a constant reminder of the eternal principles of nature, and even the smallest tree or shrub reveals something of the laws of life. If a person can grasp the laws of life in microcosm, he feels as if he can control them.

In their endeavor to realize the universe in the reduced world of miniature trees and plants, Japanese eventually discovered a whole new world in what they had created, and they sought ways to express that world. Their artistic pursuits focused on giving form to the history, life, and legends of mankind in the smallest space possible. Netsuke are one of the products of that endeavor. But while any man-made, material object is necessarily limited, the power of conceptualization is unbounded. With that insight, the idea emerged that all objects in the universe, no matter how small, are endowed with an infinite universe of their own, and that all manifestations of reality are expressions of the universe.

Transforming the face of things is another notable propensity in the Japanese life-style. A single space may be adopted to all manner of uses and occasions; a simple tool or accessory of everyday use may be manipulated for totally different purposes. Their way of life continually oriented to the cycle of the seasons, Japanese periodically alter the rhythms of their lives, responding sensitively to the movements of the seasons. Change is the very essence of nature, the basic principle of all life. What does not change does not exist. Through change, the value of an entity is established. Even space is never static; it may associate with the larger space around it, or with smaller spaces, and though there may be subdivisions of space, it is essentially continuous. Time flows on without interruption, and in response, space changes and varies its expression. Japanese have refined the modes and expressions of space to an unparalleled degree, to the point that they can even transform its nature from informal and ordinary (*ke*) to hallowed or special (*hare*), and to reflect the turn of the seasons.

Humanity and the things associated with human life are subject to constant change. All movement, from static to dynamic, from microcosm to macrocosm, from *hare* to *ke*, and from natural to artificial, is change. Through change, man seeks to affirm his existence.

Folding

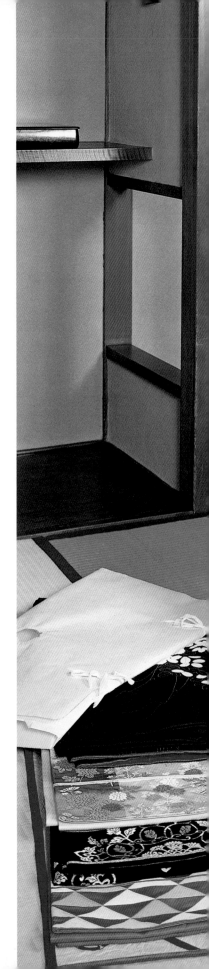

Although kimono today are generally not worn except for formal occasions, some women like this lady in Kyoto still favor the traditional mode of attire. A kimono is made from a single roll of cloth that can vary in length but never in width. Unlike the three-dimensional western dress, the kimono is flat and symmetrical, and there is only one correct way to fold it if it is to fit snugly in the drawer of a *tansu* (chest of drawers) whose specifications, in turn, match the units of measurements by which traditional houses are built. Folding reduces space to only a fraction needed for a western wardrobe.

The lady shown here has placed a *"tato-o"*—a piece of special paper—on the *tatami* floor to guard against soiling. On her right, placed by other kimono which have already been folded, is another *"tato-o"* used to individually wrap silk kimono before placing in a *tansu* for protection against dust.

和顔
愛法

If Japanese-style living makes it possible to use the same room for both living and sleeping, it is because Japanese store their bedding in closets when not in use. Shown here on the upper shelf of the closet is a set of *futon*. A *futon* is made of cotton padding encased in a cover of silk or a less expensive material. The bottom two *futon* in the closet are laid on the *tatami* floor and serve as mattresses. The top two are the equivalent of eiderdowns or blankets. A good set of *futon* costs between ¥500,000 and ¥1,000,000.

In the lower half of the closet are *zabuton* (seating mats) for day use by guests—the left set for summer and the right for winter. In Japanese, everything comes in sets of five.

Lanterns are said to have originated in China, but it was the Japanese who designed them to fold flat, accordion-like, when not in use. Made of pleated paper pasted over a frame of split bamboo, they were first used only for religious services, but soon became an essential item in daily life. Used to light doorways, decorate shop fronts, or provide vision for travellers at night, lanterns—called *chochin* by the Japanese—usually had the name of the crest of its owner painted on its side.

The paper for lanterns for outside use was durable despite their fragile appearance. Foldability not only saved space. It also made the candles inside easy to light.

Instead of wood of which Chinese screens are made, Japanese screens are made of paper and were originally intended to provide protection against draft. Since then, they have come to be used as room dividers and, like the gold-leaf screen shown here, as a movable backdrop to "set the stage" for the occasion at hand.

Lightweight and foldable, the same screen (left) can be stored with ease in a minimum of space (right).

Folding screens have from two to eight panels, but six is the most popular.

Umbrellas have changed little with time in shape or function. The changes have been in the materials used—from bamboo and oil paper, in the case of Japan, to metal and cloth—as well as in design.

The most important design change has been to make umbrellas easier to carry. Shown here is one of the smallest umbrellas today, a triple-fold model that shrinks to a length of 20 centimeters—compact enough to be carried in a ladies handbag.

In a country with as much rain as Japan, an umbrella has always been as much of one's person as a hat or a footwear.

Stacking

Stacking to save space is one thing. When stacking combines beauty and elegance with function, it can produce results like the one shown in this photograph of five graduated saké cups placed on an elevated black tray.

Made in the early 19th century and considered one of the finest works of its kind, the lacquer set, including the black dice on the side, was used at formal tea ceremonies by guests who were required to use the cup matching the face of the dice they rolled.

Each cup has a different picture. The pictures on four of the cups represent the seasons, with the smallest cup being spring. The largest cup represents love. The sixth face of the dice was a catch-all marked "others," and required the roller to perform a song or dance.

The game helped elevate drinking to a more sophisticated level, as did the conversation stimulated by the pictures and the artists who drew them.

The basic unit for the tea ceremony is five guests, hence five cups.

The lacquer trays in front of the guests in the tea ceremony scene shown here are called "fuchidaka" meaning a "high rim" which fits into the rim of the tray below to interlock for stacking.

A single cake is placed in each tray. The stacked set is first placed before the guest of honor (the man at the left) who is seated nearest the "tokonoma." He lifts the top four trays and passes them to the guest next to him, keeping the bottom tray for himself. The procedure is repeated until all five guests have their trays. The cake must be eaten before the tea is served.

Sushi—one of the most popular Japanese foods—must fulfill two functions. It must appeal to the diner's palate, and it must be attractively presented. In addition, take-out orders must be made easy to carry, for except for urban centers the bulk of the nation's *sushi* business is home delivery.

Sushi-oke—the shallow tubs of lacquered wood, but now mostly plastic—fulfill both purposes. Made in various shapes and sizes, they set off a tastefully arranged serving of *sushi* to the best advantage. And stacking makes it possible to deliver large orders, as well as save in *sushi* shops that usually have little more than a counter to serve dine-out customers.

Japanese originally used individual trays for meals instead of a central table. And since Japanese sit on *tatami* mats, it was necessary that the trays have legs not only so the diner would not have to stoop to reach his food but also to keep the food away from the floor.

The legs also permit the trays to be stacked and carried with their portions of food already in place.

Japanese inns, which have no dining rooms, still use legged-trays to serve guests in their rooms with the two daily meals—breakfast and dinner—included in the price of Japanese-style accommodation.

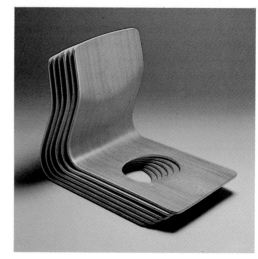

Dictionaries define a *za-isu* as a "legless chair used in a *tatami* room." Essentially, it is a back-rest for people who need support when sitting Japanese-style, as many foreigners have discovered to their relief at Japanese banquets.

However, *za-isu*—a relatively recent invention—were developed for the benefit for the Japanese themselves, many of whom, in adopting western living styles, find they no longer have the muscles needed to squat on the floor. Whether the back of the *za-isu* is rigid or hinged, it can be easily stacked for storage.

Rolling

Rolling as a means of saving space is almost as old as human history. But few civilizations have applied rolling to as many purposes as the Japanese.

One of the reasons rolling was so widely practiced in ancient Japan was the resilient quality of traditional Japanese rice paper. Until recently, letters were written on rolled paper, which could be cut to the length of the epistle.

Scrolls of pictures or calligraphy that decorate the *tokonoma* (alcoves) of Japanese rooms are rolled and unrolled time and again without damage.

In addition to saving space, rolling up a scroll protects it from dust, dampness and light. For further protection it was placed in a wooden box made from cedar wood. Such boxes, often lacquered and tied with a silk cord, were the standard mode for hand-carrying letters between persons of high rank. The custom of rolling continues to this day in the use of tube-like containers for diplomas and certificates.

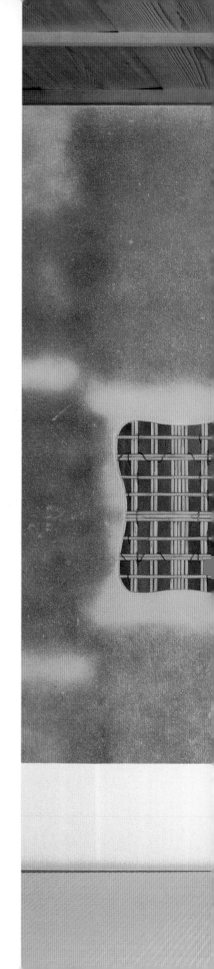

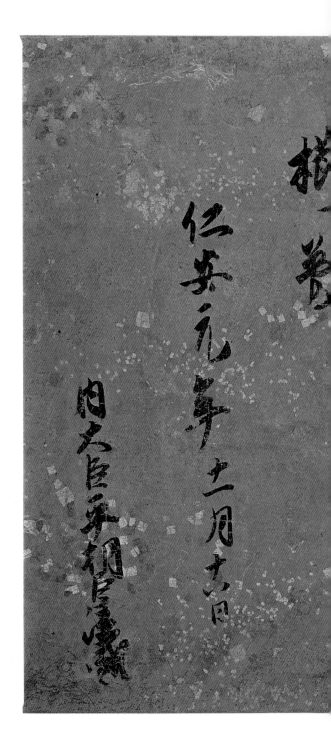

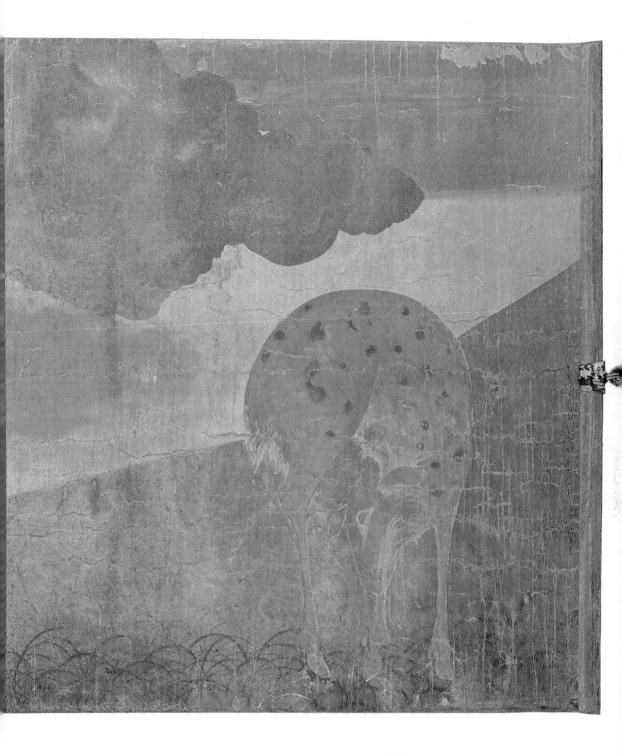

Of the many types of ancient scrolls, none was more revered than the hand scrolls on which Buddhist sutras were written. Among the most famous of these is the "Heike Nokyo," a section of which is shown here. Produced in 1164, its beauty lies not only in the orderly line up of the characters but in the comprehensive design of the religíous pictures and the decorative binding.

There are several reasons for rolling a bolt of kimono cloth, or an obi (sash). It prevents creasing and protects the material. The bolts can be placed on top of each other for storage without shelves. And they are easy to show to customers, for the bolt simply has to be unrolled a few meters to display its design and texture.

Bolts of kimono are all the same size—11 meters long and 36 centimeters wide—but can be made up to fit anybody. Height adjustments are made by tucking up the kimono at the waist. The best kimonos are still made of pure silk, as are obi, whose width varys according to purpose.

Obi, whose history is shorter than that of the kimono, first appeared in the 8th century to replace hemp cords then in use. It wasn't until the 15th century, however, that women's obi became wider and more decorative than men's.

The *sudare* is a shade made of thin reeds or split bamboo woven together with string, and is used for both decorative and practical purposes.

Hung inside Japanese homes, it serves as a room divider and improves ventilation.

Hung in front of windows or doors, it also offers privacy and protection from the sun. The *sudare*'s versatility is enhanced by the fact that it can be rolled to any desired length to suit the occasion.

Of the items of equipment that the man be-hind the counter at a *sushi* shop must have to prepare his wares, none is more impor-tant than a small, simple mat 27 centimeters by 24 centimeters made of split bamboo.

Called a *sunoko*, it is what he uses to roll *maki-zushi*, as opposed to the variety of *sushi* in which the raw fish, or whatever delicacy the diner fancies, is placed on top of one-mouthful servings of rice.

Maki-zushi means "hand-rolled *sushi.*" The *sunoko* is laid flat and a sheet of seaweed is placed on it. Then a portion of cooked rice is spread over the seaweed, after which various ingredients (egg, cucumber, gourd shavings, etc.) are placed across the center of the rice. With everything in place, the end of the *sunoko* is lifted and folded over to press the ingredients into a neat roll that is cut into sections for serving. Although sea-weed is the most used "wrapping" for the roll, a sheet of egg prepared to resemble a thick pancake is also popular.

Though making *maki-zushi* is a simply pro-cess to watch, it is a technique that requires considerable experience.

Nesting

Boxes like these are still used in Japan today for measuring liquids and solids in traditional Japanese units. The boxes here—called *masu*—are made from natural, unpainted wood and are for measuring grain, as opposed to boxes for measuring liquids which are coated with lacquer to prevent the liquid from seeping into the wood.

The largest *masu* holds one *sho* of liquid (1800 cc), and the smallest holds one *shaku* (18 cc). In between is the measurement of one *go.* Ten *shaku* equals one *go,* and ten *go* equals one *sho.*

In feudal Japan tribute was paid to feudal lords in rice which was measured in units of *masu.* Thus the size of the *masu* determined the amount of tribute, and sizes varied considerably among the many fiefdoms throughout the country.

Toyotomi Hideyoshi (1536 – 98) was the first to establish a nationwide standard for *masu.* Two *masu*-makers were appointed to produce all the *masu* for the whole of Japan.

Their *masu* were branded with their seals, and any *masu* lacking them was illegal. These two families and their descendants remained the only authorized *masu* makers for 200 years until 1875 when new modern standards were established.

In feudal Japan, a picnic was an elaborate affair that required much preparation, not the least of which was readying the picnic lunch. Several lunch boxes were prepared, each with different kinds of food. But the boxes were graded in size so that on the journey home they could be placed one inside the next to be reduced to a single box that was easy to carry.

Such lunch box sets were called *ireko bento*, *ireko* suggesting the placing of something small into something larger. The term *bento*, meaning box lunch, is still used today.

The *ireko* concept also found expression in other ways related to food, such as in the "husband and wife" pair of tea cups with the wife's always smaller so that it fitted into the husband's, or in the alms bowls of graded size carried by Zen Buddhist monks.

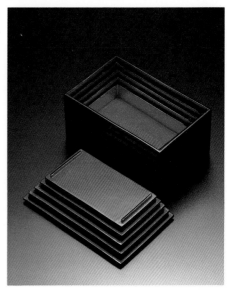

These alms bowls, graded in size to nest in a set, are used at a restaurant in Kyoto specializing in Zen Buddhist vegetarian food. Japanese Buddhist priests and novices begging alms carry alms bowls in sets of three to six in graded sizes.

Eventually, restaurants featuring Buddhist food began to appear, and to add authenticity they used dishes shaped like alms bowls.

Although monks originally used alms bowls made of metal or ceramics, those made for restaurants today are made from lacquered wood.

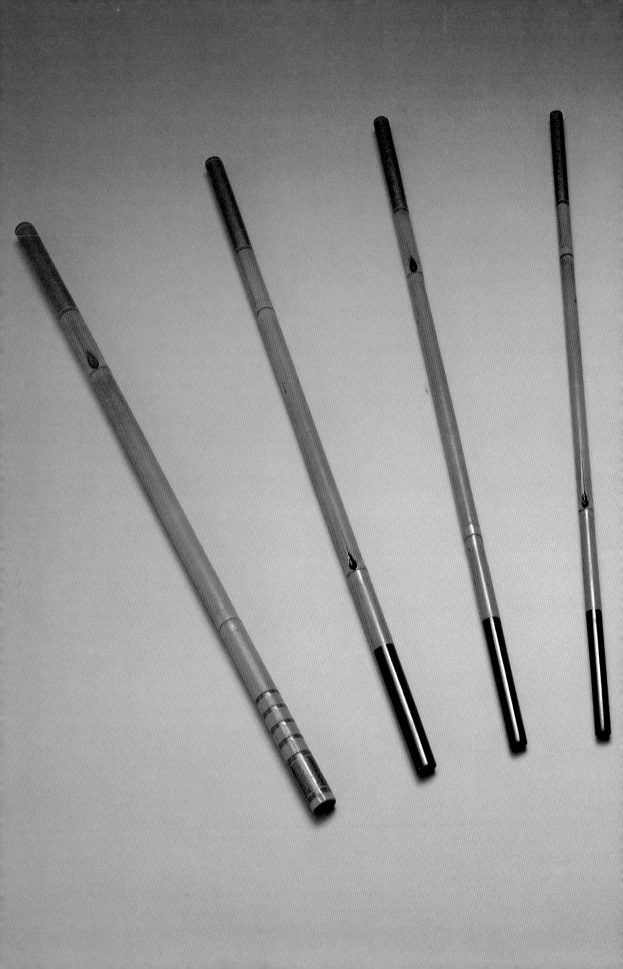

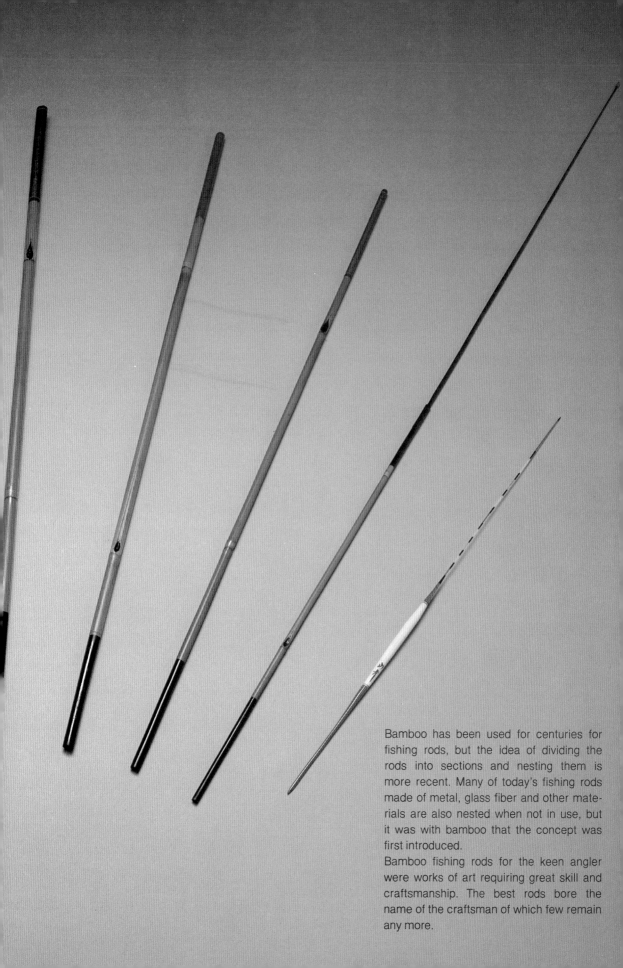

Bamboo has been used for centuries for fishing rods, but the idea of dividing the rods into sections and nesting them is more recent. Many of today's fishing rods made of metal, glass fiber and other materials are also nested when not in use, but it was with bamboo that the concept was first introduced.

Bamboo fishing rods for the keen angler were works of art requiring great skill and craftsmanship. The best rods bore the name of the craftsman of which few remain any more.

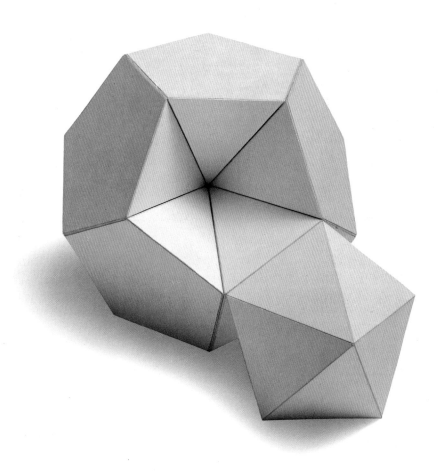

From the cubic dodecahedron at left, the
hinged polyhedrons from which it is formed
can be rearranged to produce a fascinating
variety of shapes, two of which are shown
here. Both are creations of the topological
artist Tomura Hiroshi. The top is titled
"Dragon" and the bottom "Star." According
to Plato, the dodecahedron symbolized the
universe, the octahedron was the wind, the
tetrahedron cube was fire, and the icosa-
hedron cube represented water.

Carrying

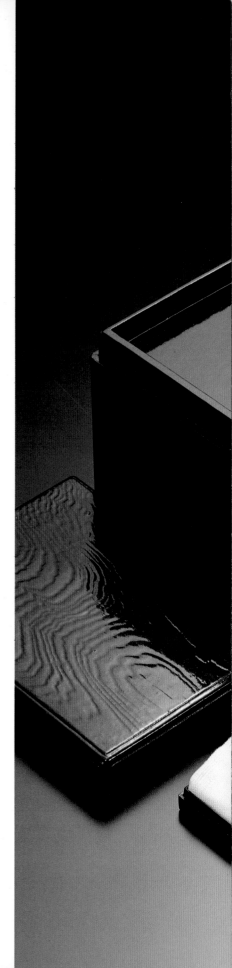

The extent to which the tea ceremony was an essential part of cultural life among the educated classes in feudal Japan is indicated in these photographs of a portable set of utensils that made it possible to perform this esoteric art almost anywhere. Although the normal place for the tea ceremony was in a special room in the home designed and set aside for this purpose, it was also performed out-of-doors at picnics, or during one's travels at wherever one happened to be staying. For such occasions, portable, self-contained sets were made. The equipment was carried in a box generally no more than 21 centimeters long and 14 centimeters wide, and 13 centimeters deep.

Generally made of lacquered cedar wood, the bottom part of the box was for the larger objects such as the tea cup, the tea powder container and bamboo whisk, while the upper part, fitted with a shallow tray, was for the smaller utensils.

Tea made and served with portable equipment was a much more informal event than the ritualized ceremony called for under classical rules of conduct proscribed by the masters of the art.

Of the items a traveller in feudal Japan was required to take with him on his journey, two of the most essential were a portable pillow (*tabi-makura*) and a writing brush case (*yatate*). Pillows were hard and high which was necessary so the head rested on it at the base of the skull without messing up the elaborate style of the time. This also allowed them to be made like wooden boxes in which the traveller could pack personal items. Compactly arranged, the items included everything from a bedside lantern to an abacus, mirror, wallet, sewing kit and other miscellaneous objects. The *yatate* shown in the photograph with the pillow holds a brush in its handle and a cotton-like substance soaked with ink at the end. It was developed in the Kamakura period (1192–1333) and continued in use until the introduction of the pen in the Meiji Restoration.

Of the different varieties of picnic lunch boxes in feudal Japan, the most elaborate was that used on flower-viewing outings. Flower-viewing was a special event, and picnic sets for such occasions were often carefully crafted works of art.

Functionally, the box was a carrying case for bottles of saké, food and eating utensils. But from the Momoyama period (1573–1603) they began to be lacquered and decorated lavishly with designs in gold dust. As they became a vehicle of the highest technical and artistic expression of lacquer craftsmen, they were made in a wide variety of shapes of grace and beauty.

Modern lunch jars have transformed the cold box lunch into an appetizing hot meal. Thermos-type lunch jars, neatly packed with a variety of hot dishes, are a favorite with carpenters, plumbers and others in the building trade, as well as picnickers, campers, hunters, fishermen—almost anyone preferring a home-cooked meal in an age of instant foods and vending machines. Thermos lunch jars range in cost from ¥4,000 to ¥8,000.

Transistor radios made sound a portable item, but ICs and stereo technology have given it a new dimension. Stereo sound from radios and cassettes small enough to snap onto a belt or put in a handbag transport the listener into his own private world through light headphones. The most avid fans of portable stereo cassette players are the younger generation who find it a way to spend their time commuting to school or work.

Consolidating

Shown here is an exquisite set of utensils made in the 17th century by Igarashi Doho, the famous artisan of gold-lacquer ware, for use in an incense game that was played by the Japanese aristocracy. Consisting of incense burners, tools to prepare the incense, incense packages, markers, a marker box and other items, everything fitted compactly into a lacquered box when not in use.

Basically, the game was to identify various varieties of incense by their aroma.

Although the Japanese had developed an appreciation for incense as early as the Heian period (794–1185), it was not until the 15th century that incense-guessing became a game with fixed rules.

During the Edo period (1603–1868), attention came to be paid as much to the beauty of the equipment used as to the game's competitive aspects.

There were many variations of the game which could be made easier or more difficult by reducing or increasing the varieties of incense. Each player had a marker which was moved progressively towards the finishing line as each incense was correctly identified.

In the west, the space under stairways is often used as a closet. In Japanese homes, the space was frequently used for built-in drawers. Stairs with built-in drawers were placed as a rule to provide access to the attic. Thus, the stairs themselves were used only occasionally, for example, to bring down an extra set of dishes for guests, or replace a folding screen, since attics were the only storage area in Japanese homes. But the drawers were filled with items of daily use, such as writing paper, envelopes, pins, scissors and other bric-a-brac.

Hako-kaidan (box stairway) is one of the several names by which they were called. The making and installation of a *Hako-kaidan* required the skills of both carpenter and cabinet maker.

This impressive *funa-dansu* (sea chest) was used in the late Edo period to transport money aboard ship in coastal commerce.

Funa-dansu were designed with various devices to foil would-be thieves. In the *funa-dansu* shown here, what looks like the upper drawer is actually a panel removed by lifting to reveal what appear to be three smaller drawers, whose fronts also must be removed to reach the money boxes inside. The bottom section has similar fake drawers. Even the supports separating the drawers are designed to conceal private documents. This *funa-dansu* has a total of 15 locks and holds six money boxes called *senryo-bako* each containing 1,000 pieces of gold.

This *naga-hibachi* is typical of the multi-function charcoal brazier used for centuries in Japanese homes. Its place was the *cha-no-ma*, the communal room that served as a combination living room-dining room where the family gathered or invited close friends. The charcoal was kept burning all day, in the *naga-hibachi.*

An iron kettle always placed over the fire for tea and warming saké for family members and guests.

In addition to heating, the brazier served as a stove or grill for light edibles.

A third function was a table, for which the top of the *naga-hibachi* was extended on one side (right side in the photograph). The extended side has a hole concealed with a flat cover into which charcoal not completely burned was placed at night to be extinguished by lack of air for re-use the next day. The extended side was popularly called *neko-ita*, meaning cat's board, for cats liked to rest on its warmth.

The drawers at the bottom fulfilled the fourth and fifth functions—as a deposit for valuables, and as a place where small objects could be dried by the heat reflected from the burning charcoal.

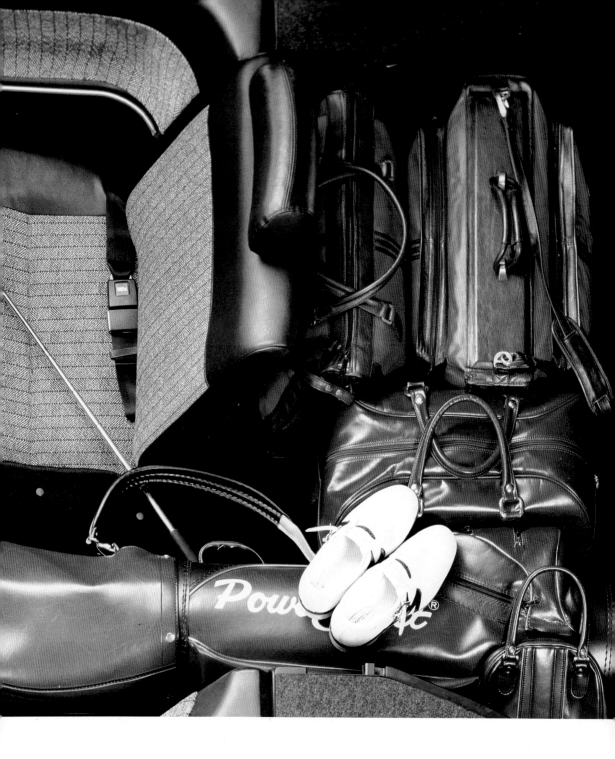

The art of making the most of the least today plays an important function in automobile design as well.

The back of the rear seat of this compact, five-passenger hatchback folds forward on one or both sides to accommodate extra luggage. Folded on one side, as shown here, it seats three persons and allows maximum use of the extra space for luggage too big for the trunk.

Miniaturizing

Doll displays on Girls' Day, March 3 are a centuries-old custom in Japan. But miniature dolls originated as talisman. In the Heian period (794–1185) members of the nobility made miniature dolls and cast them into the river or sea in March to carry away evil spirits. From these beginnings, the dolls took on symbolic meaning, as objects through which to pray for a child's health and happiness, or for parents to pray for children away from home.

In the Edo period (1603–1868), the custom of displaying dolls on Girls' Day grew in popularity, and the displays became more elaborate. In place of simple dolls accompanied by simple offerings of wine, fish or rice-cakes, the displays came to symbolize court life, featuring the emperor and empress and their attendants, court musicians (who were increased in number as the displays became more elaborate), and miniatures of various implements of court life. The doll set in this photograph is one of the most lavish in existence. It was made in the late 19th century for the daughter of the feudal lord Mohri as part of her dowry.

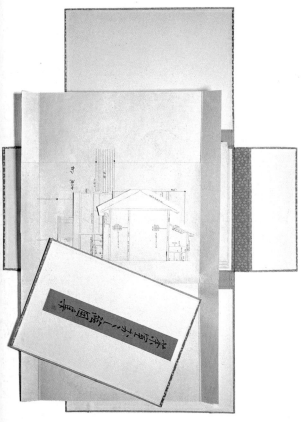

One of the most unusual examples of space-saving in feudal Japan is to be found in the paper replicas of Japanese tea houses commissioned by the 18th century feudal lord Matsudaira Sadanobu (1758–1829). Shown here is a rare copy of the replica of the Teigyoku-ken tea house in the Shinju-an living quarters of Daitokuji temple in Kyoto. It is one of 50 famous tea houses in Japan as a reference for those who wanted to build their own tea houses along similar lines. The walls, with windows and other details drawn in, are pasted to the floor and raised vertically to provide a three-dimensional miniature of the tea house. When not in use, the walls are folded flat in a compact, two-dimensional package.

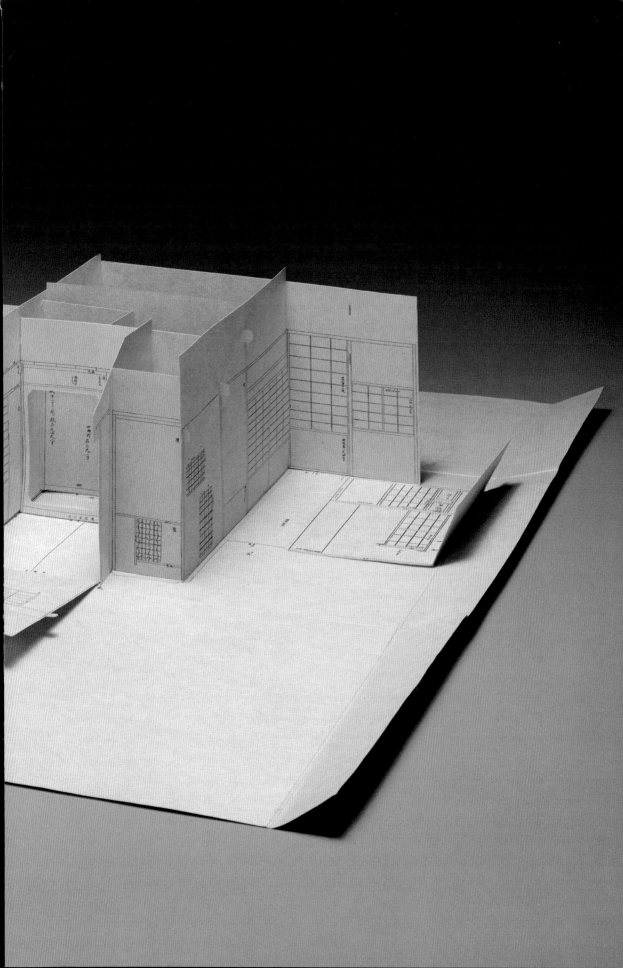

If Japanese are naturally dextrous with their hands, the trait was exhibited in feudal Japan no better than in netsuke—the small, elaborately hand-carved objects attached to the strings of a pouch to hold it in place on the sash around the waist.

Made from ivory, hardwood, metal, stone or lacquer, no two netsuke are alike. For they were carved to order with designs of figures, animals, plants, masks, or whatever the customer fancied. Popular design themes included the animal of the year of the zodiac in which the wearer was born, images of the famous priest Dharma, popular heroes, legendary figures, and masks.

The growing of bonsai—miniature potted trees and plants—has been practiced in Japan for centuries. By pruning, wiring, and a great deal of care and patience, nature is reproduced in miniature. Some bonsai are over 100 years old, conveying the full range of reactions the viewer would have to the object in its natural size and environment which, after all, is the aim of this highly-developed art.

More-recently, there has emerged a boom in mini-bonsai of plants and trees small enough to fit on the palm of the hand. Displays of mini-bonsai like the one shown at left are a common sight today.

Japanese express their love of nature in many ways. One that has been practiced for over 1,000 years is *bonkei*, which literally translates as "landscape on a tray."

The purpose of *bonkei* is to reproduce in miniature a landscape real or imagined within the confines of a tray that is no more than 40 centimeters wide.

Using rocks, miniature trees, moss, sand, small houses, figurines and whatever other material lends itself to the total picture in the creator's mind, *bonkei* is usually not a permanent work of art, especially when live plants are used.

Whereas bonsai (miniature trees) last sometimes over 100 years, the beauty of *bonkei* is ephemeral.

102

Transforming

A pair of chopsticks is the simplest of utensils with a wide variety of uses. Chopsticks, in their simplicity and versatility, are a basic representation of Japanese culture. There is no Japanese food served that cannot be eaten with chopsticks. In fact, those accustomed to chopsticks prefer them over western eating utensils, especially for such tasks as picking fish clean from the bone, lifting peas, lifting just the right amount of rice from the bowl for a mouthful, or even mixing dough.

Chopsticks vary in shape and material depending upon their use. Chopsticks for New Year are made of willow. For exclusive *kaiseki*-style dinner parties, they are made from freshly-cut green bamboo with both ends tapered—one end for fish and the other for vegetable. Other, more durable woods are preferred for daily use, while expensive chopsticks are made from ivory. And then there are the *wari-bashi*, or the one-piece chopsticks found in restaurants and box lunches that are split into two for use.

The *tenugui* is a piece of cotton cloth about 90 centimeters long and 33 centimeters wide that serves many functions—as a towel, handkerchief, scarf, to wrap around the head, to mention only some of its uses. *Tenugui* became popular with the rise of the merchant class in the 18th century. They were originally made of ramie and were somewhat longer than *tenugui* used today, for they were also used as banners or sashes. With the cultivation of cotton in the Edo period, cotton became the preferred material. It also became a popular gift, dyed with crests and designs publicising the donor or his business. *Tenugui* are still widely used today, especially as gifts.

And all inns offer *tenugui* to their guests to serve as both face towels and bath towels in the Japanese tradition.

In the photographs, the man dressed in a traditional fireman's coat illustrates the many ways a *tenugui* can be worn on the head.

Bukkaeri, meaning quick costume change technique, performed by the *Kabuki* actor at the climax of the drama to transform himself from one character into another. The actor here is Onoe Shoroku who plays the role of Narukami, a saintly priest who becomes enraged to learn that he has been deceived by a beautiful woman named Kumo-no-Taemahime.

To make the change from saintliness to rage he pulls a string on his garment that transforms it into a fire-flame pattern.

Japanese rooms are modular in design, like
this illustration of the interior of Edo Castle
which shows several rooms whose *fusuma*
doors have been removed to make a single,
large banquet hall.

The photographs on the previous page
show the same room.

Through the use of paper *shoji* and paper
fusuma doors in winter, and *sudare shoji*,
split bamboo *fusuma* and *tomushiro* (split
rattan) floor covering in summer, Japanese
rooms can be adapted to the seasons.

Mountains, rivers, all things living
pay homage to the whims of the seasons
in their eternal cycle.

Seisei, 1869−1937

Notes

• Covers
Paper folding fan
Courtesy of "Tomatsu-ya Fukui Tobei,"
Kyoto.
Photographs by Hatakeyama Takashi.
• 8
Senmai-da (thousands rice paddies)
Photograph courtesy of Boncolor
Photo Agency.
• 10
Shinto ground-breaking
Courtesy of Takenaka Komuten Co., Ltd.
Photograph by Kohno Yutaka.
• 12
The garden of Kinkaku-ji temple, Kyoto
Muromachi period, 15th century.
Courtesy of Kinkaku-ji temple.
Photograph by Iwamiya Takeji.
• 16
Suiseki (water stone), "Yamato Murayama"
Collection of Rai Sanyo (1781 – 1832).
Courtesy of the Rai Sanyo Kyuseki Hozon-kai.
Photograph by Hatakeyama Takashi.
• 18
Kaishi paper
Photograph by Iwamiya Takeji.
• 20
New Year decorations
Courtesy of "Nakazato," Kyoto.
Photograph by Iwamiya Takeji.
• 23
Miniature stupa
Nara period, 764 – 70.
Wood covered with gesso.
H. 21.8 cm; Diam. of base 10.5 cm.
Important Cultural Property.
Photograph courtesy of Tokyo National
Museum.

• 25 (see page 24)
"The Mandala of Japanese Dualism"
Drawing by Yoshida Mitsukuni.
• 33
Shukkei-en, Hiroshima
The very name of this garden—Shukkei-en,
meaning a garden of reduced landscape—
indicates the intent of its builder, the 17th
century feudal lord Asano, who conceived
it as a miniaturized reproduction of a
famous lake scene in China. It was built in
1620 in what is now Hiroshima.
Destroyed by the atom bomb in 1945, the
garden was rebuilt, and providing proof that
even severe radioactivity cannot prevent
the recreation of nature's vegetation.
Courtesy of Hiroshima prefecture.
Photograph by Hatakeyama Takashi.

Folding
• 34 – 35
Kimono
Courtesy of "Tsurui," Gion in Kyoto.
Photographs by Hatakeyama Takashi.
• 36 – 37
Futon bedding
Courtesy of Hatta Shinso K.K., Kyoto.
Photographs by Hatakeyama Takashi.
• 38 – 39
Paper lantern
Lanterns at the Gion Festival.
Courtesy of the Usui residence,
Gion in Kyoto.
Photographs by Hatakeyama Takashi.
• 40 – 41
Golden screen
Courtesy of Mitsukoshi Silver House, Tokyo.
Photographs by Hirokawa Taishi.

Isaburo, cabinet-maker in Kyoto.
Courtesy of "Enami," Kyoto.
Photographs by Hatakeyama Takashi.
• 66 – 67
Ireko bento (nested lunch boxes)
Collection of Kida Yasuhiko.
Meals prepared by "Sakamoto," Gion
in Kyoto.
Photographs by Hatakeyama Takashi.
• 68 – 69
Alms bowls
Courtesy of "Izusen," Kyoto.
Photographs by Hatakeyama Takashi.
• 70 – 71
Fishing rods
Collection of Ekuan Kenji.
Photograph by Sakuma Nobumitsu.
• 72 – 73
Dodecahedron "Stars and Dragon"
by Tomura Hiroshi.
Photographs by Sakuma Nobumitsu.

Carrying
• 74 – 75
Chabako (box of tea utensils)
Lacquerwork by Ikkan XIV.
Collection of Nakamura Hiroko.
Photographs by Hatakeyama Takashi.
• 76 – 77
Tabi-makura (pillow box for travelling) and
yatate (a portable brush-and-ink case)
Edo period, 18th century.
Collection of National Institute of Japanese
Literature, Tokyo.
Photographs by Sakuma Nobumitsu.
• 78 – 79
Hanami bento
(lunch boxes for flower viewing)

Edo period, 18th century.
Collection of Tamaki Hambei.
Photograph by Azuma Shoji.
• 80 – 81
"Lunch jar" thermos bottle
Courtesy of Zojirushi Vacuum Bottle
Co., Ltd.
Photograph by Hirokawa Taishi.
Lunch jar, first appeared on market in
Japan around 1973. Annual production
today ranges from 1.5 million to 2 million.
Most are for the domestic market, and
some are exported to South East Asia and
Central and South America.
Source: All-Japan Vacuum Bottle
Association.
• 82 – 83
Headphone stereo sets; National "World Way"
stereo cassette players
Courtesy of Matsushita Electric Industrial
Co., Ltd.
Photograph by Hirokawa Taishi.

Consolidating
• 84 – 85
Set of utensils for the incense game with
autumn grass design
Early Edo period, 17th century.
Lacquerwork by Doho.
Photographs by Hatakeyama Takashi.
• 86 – 87
Hako-kaidan (box stairway)
Courtesy of the "Yoshida-ya," Kyoto.
Photograph by Hatakeyama Takashi.
• 88 – 89
Sea chest
Japan Folkcraft Museum Collection.
Photographs by Sakuma Nobumitsu.

• 90 – 91
Naga-hibachi (oblong brazier)
Courtesy of Yagi Akira, Kyoto.
Photograph by Hatakeyama Takashi.
• 92 – 93
The luggage compartment of MAZDA 323
Nowhere has greater attention been paid in
modern times to getting the most out of a
limited amount of space than in the
automobile industry. One of the most
successful developments in this regard has
been the front-wheel drive which, in
addition to reducing power loss, has
provided more room for rear passengers
and the luggage compartment.
The MAZDA 323 (the MAZDA GLC in the
United States) was chosen "'80 – '81 Car
of the Year in Japan."
With engine, transmission and differential
gears fitted compactly under the hood, it
offers exceptional roominess, plus rear
seats that fold down for extra utility space
when needed.

Miniaturizing

• 94 – 95
Hina doll display
Collection of Bunka Gakuen Fukushoku
Hakubutsukan (Costume Museum), Tokyo.
Photograph courtesy of Heibonsha Limited,
Publishers.
• 96 – 97
Chashitsu-Okoshi-Ezu (raised and
assembled picture of tea rooms)
From the "Collection of *Chashitsu-Okoshi-
Ezu*—Cubic Patterns of Japanese Tea-
Room" published by the Bokusui Publishing
Co., Ltd. These paper replicas of 50 tea-

rooms were reproduced under the
supervision of Dr. Horiguchi Sutemi.
Title calligraphy by Shinoda Toko.
Collection of Shinoda Toko.
Photographs by Sakuma Nobumitsu.
• 98 – 99
Netsuke and *inro*
The pouch to whose strings the netsuke
was attached was usually an *inro*, originally
used to carry seals but later as an
accessory to carry pills and other small
personal objects for which a kimono had
no pockets.
Tokyo National Museum Collection.
Photographs courtesy of Tokyo National
Museum.
• 100 – 101
Mini-bonsai
Courtesy of Ginza Mitsukoshi Department
Store.
Photographs by Sakuma Nobumitsu.
• 102 – 103
Bonkei (landscape on a tray)
Eight *bonkei* shown are works by the
members of the Nippon Bonkei Society.
Photographs courtesy of Seibun-do
Shinko-sha.

Transforming

• 104 – 105
Chopsticks
Courtesy of the "Homasa," Tokyo.
Photographs by Hirokawa Taishi.
• 106 – 107
Tenugui towel
Modelled by "Tobi-Gin" Ikeda Ginichi.
Courtesy of "Fuji-ya," Asakusa, Tokyo.
Photographs by Hirokawa Taishi.

- 108 – 109

Bukkaeri (quick costume change)
Onoe Shoroku in role of Narukami in
Kabuki play "Narukami."
Photographs by Hayashi Kakichi.

- 110 – 111

Interiors of a Japanese house
Courtesy of the Nakamura Sotetsu
residence, Kyoto.
Photographs by Hatakeyama Takashi.

- 112

Doroe (gouache painting) "Interior of
Edo Castle"
Late Edo period, 19th century.
Japan Folkcraft Museum Collection.
Photograph courtesy of Japan Folkcraft
Museum.

- 113

This haiku (17-syllable poem) represents
poetry at its most compact. The poet,
Matsuse Seisei, was born in Osaka in 1869.
A leading exponent of haiku, he also
excelled at calligraphy and painting.

Text by Yoshida Mitsukuni,
translated by the staff of the
Center for Social Science Communication
Captions by the editorial staff

Editor: Sesoko Tsune
Art Director: Tanaka Ikko
Designer: Kinoshita Katsuhiro
Editorial Supervisor: Ken Ishii
Editorial Assistants: Mizukami Machiko
        Kondoh Ryuji
        Kobayashi Akemi
        Sawada Naoko

Printed by Dai Nippon Printing Co., Ltd.
Printed in Japan